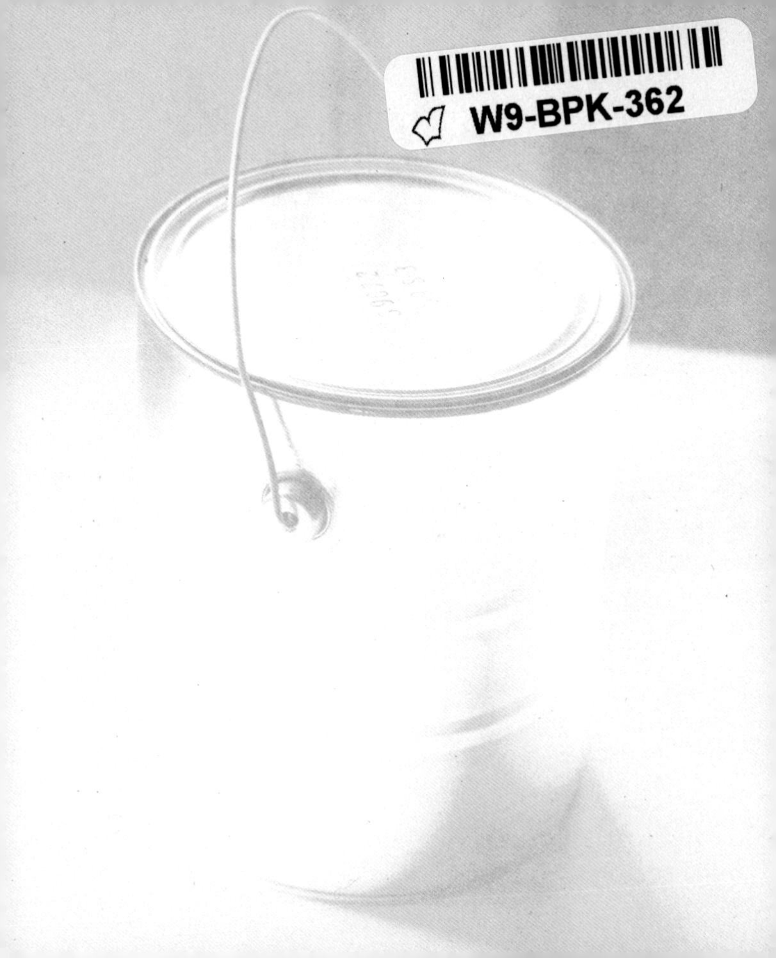

CHIC

SIMPLE ™

Components

"If I didn't start painting,
I would have raised chickens."

GRANDMA MOSES

CHIC

SIMPLE ™

Components

P A I N T

room to room

ALFRED A. KNOPF   NEW YORK   1994

THIS IS A BORZOI BOOK
PUBLISHED BY ALFRED A. KNOPF, INC.

Copyright © 1994 by Chic Simple,
a partnership of
A Stonework, Ltd., and Kim Johnson Gross, Inc.

All rights reserved under International and Pan-American Copyright
Conventions. Published in the United States by Alfred A. Knopf, Inc., New York,
and simultaneously in Canada by Random House of Canada Limited, Toronto.
Distributed by Random House, Inc., New York.

KIM JOHNSON GROSS   JEFF STONE

WRITTEN BY TODD LYON
PHOTOGRAPHS BY MARIA ROBLEDO
STYLED BY HANNAH MILMAN
COLOR CONSULTING & ART BY EVE ASHCRAFT

DESIGN AND ART DIRECTION BY
ROBERT VALENTINE INCORPORATED

ICON ILLUSTRATION BY ERIC HANSON

Library of Congress Cataloging-in-Publication Data
Lynn, Todd.
Chic Simple: Paint/Kim Johnson Gross, Jeff Stone,
Todd Lyon. — 1st ed.
p. cm. — (Chic Simple)
ISBN 0-679-43217-6
1. House painting. 2. Color in interior decoration. I. Title. II. Series.
TT323.L96 1994
698'.14–dc20
94-4622
CIP

Grateful acknowledgment is made to EMI Music Publishing for permission to
reprint an excerpt from "Fixing a Hole" by John Lennon and Paul McCartney,
copyright © 1967 by Northern Songs Ltd. All rights controlled and administered
by EMI Blackwood Music, Inc., under license from ATV Music Corp. (MacLen
Music). All rights reserved. International copyright secured. Used by permission.

Manufactured in the United States of America
First Edition

CONTENTS

"The more you know, the less you need."

AUSTRALIAN ABORIGINAL SAYING

Chic Simple is a primer for living well but sensibly. It's
for those who believe that quality of life does not come
in accumulating things, but in paring down to the
essentials. Chic Simple enables readers to bring value
and style into their lives with economy and simplicity.

P A I N T

There are few acts more primitive than painting, and few substances more primitive than paint. Ever since shapes were sketched on cave walls by some prehistoric hand, paint has been a medium for ritual and magic. It has summoned and appeased the gods, recorded history via frescoes and friezes, illuminated medieval manuscripts. In ancient China, painting embodied the spirit of Tao; in India it has depicted the lives of the Buddha; in the Americas it decorated ceremonial garments. A sacred substance, paint; a gift of color coaxed from the good earth.

> "Painting is easy when you don't know how, but very difficult when you do."
>
> EDGAR DEGAS

THE HISTORY OF PAINT
IS ABOUT THE PARALLEL PATHS OF

AESTHETIC AND UTILITARIAN NEEDS. WHILE ANCIENT

artisans ground pigment and fashioned fine brushes from animal fur,

unsung mortals used substances like tar and tree sap to protect their

homes from nature's battering. Sometime during the industrial age,

"It's my color-

beauty and utility converged: today, we protect our homes and make

them lovely at the same time. We could choose to cover our walls with

materials that never needed painting, yet we choose the labor, the

expense, and the rich possibilities of paint. With it, we make our

small environments our own, reflecting our singular personality.

GRECIAN FORMULA 432 B.C.: *The exterior of the Parthenon is embellished with bright red, blue, yellow, gold, and black accents. The paint eventually falls off, resulting in the historical misconception that classical architecture is marked by a restrained use of color.* **PRESERVATION HALL** 79 A.D.: *The Hall of Mysteries in Pompeii is painted, using lime-resistant colors over wet lime plaster, a fresco technique whose permanence is helped along by being buried in volcanic ash for 1,669 years.* **EARLY FAUX** 1500: *In Rome, nouveau-riche merchants hire artisans to decorate their country villas with imitation textiles painted on the walls.* **PILGRIM'S PROGRESS** Circa 1737: *Dutch colonists, bored with the drabness of New England, whitewash their homes and paint*

beige!"

ELSIE DE WOLFE
(on seeing the Parthenon for the first time)

their exterior trim with vivid red and green paint. Puritans disapprove. **THE MUMMY'S CURSE, REALIZED** Circa 1850: *A popular pigment sold under the name "Mummy" is abruptly taken off the market when the public discovers it's actually made from ground-up Egyptian mummies.* **BOVINE SURPRISE** 1908: *Indian Lake, a popular pigment manufactured in India by heating the urine of cows fed on mango leaves, becomes obsolete when its chemical composition is revealed to English consumers.* **REGULAR OR UNLEADED?** Circa 1942: *The U.S. Army creates a paste that, when mixed with either water or gasoline, turns into camouflage paint, but they keep losing the cans.*

"Color is my
strongest weapon:
And it's the least
expensive way to
decorate. With a
gallon of paint you
can change the
entire feeling of a
room."

MARIO BUATTA

Transformation. At our fingertips is a dazzling array of choices. We can change a room from powder blue to citron green in a single afternoon. In two or three evenings we can make our walls the color and texture of a cloak in a painting by Caravaggio. We can create an El Greco sky, a dappled wall of Provence, or pale stripes that recall Paris in the springtime. Paint can turn a formal room into a cozy retreat, and can make a small, dark corner seem airy and bright. With paint we do more than change the color of a wall: we can change the mood and context of a room.

"I'm painting the room in a colorful way,
And when my mind is wandering
there I will go."

LENNON & McCARTNEY, *"Fixing a Hole,"*
Sgt. Pepper's Lonely Hearts Club Band

Mood. Blue is cool. Red is warm. White reflects light. Black absorbs light. These scant facts are what the average person knows about the physical properties of color. But ask that same person his or her opinion about the color of a room and you'll get an earful. People respond to color on a multitude of levels—psychological, cultural, physiological. Is it all subjective? That's the question to which Faber Birren, the world's reigning colorist through the '50s, '60s, and '70s, dedicated his life. He studied how colors affect human behavior, and the results of his experiments influenced generations of paint choosers.

COLOR ACCORDING TO FABER BIRREN

1. *Red increases sexual activity, heals wounds, raises blood pressure, makes weight seem heavier, and makes time seem longer. Excellent for the creation but not the execution of ideas.* 2. *Blue decreases hormonal activity, inhibits the healing of wounds, lowers blood pressure, makes weight seem lighter, and time seem shorter. Unsuccessful in schools, offices, and hospitals.* 3. *Yellow speeds the metabolism.* 4. *Green reduces nervous and muscular tension.* 5. *Visual and mental concentration is easiest in a green, gray, or blue environment with low brightness.* 6. *Small children become relaxed in actively-colored rooms.* 7. *Peach, red, orange, brown, buff, yellow, and clear green stimulate the appetite. Pink and violet are "dessert" colors because they're perceived as being sweet.* 8. *Blondes prefer blue; brunettes prefer red.*

Simple Paint. It's old-fashioned. It doesn't last. It requires patience and odd ingredients. But for all that, what could look more natural than whitewash? It was once poor people's paint, something you could cook up in the kitchen and brush on the living room walls when visitors came from out of town. Today, we love whitewash for its simplicity, its airiness, its translucence. Whitewash never looks artificial.

TOM SAWYER'S WHITEWASH FUND
12 marbles, a kite, a dead rat, a fragment of chalk, a key, six firecrackers, a one-eyed kitten, a piece of blue bottle glass, a spool cannon, a glass stopper, a brass doorknob, two tadpoles, a dog collar, the handle of a knife, four pieces of orange peel, a window sash, part of a jew's harp, and an apple. Given by friends for the privilege of painting.

"There are plenty of books telling you that cool colors make you feel calm and warm colors make you feel cheerful and that black is not a great color for a bedroom, but I think all that is nonsense. Do what you want."

MARY ELLEN PINKHAM, *Mary Ellen's Clean House*

Geography and Light. The relationship between color and light begins with geography. In tropical countries, colors like flamingo pink, mango-yellow, and Caribbean blue are infused with white-hot light. In cold countries light is filtered through layers of mist. There, natural colors are gray-based: rust red, forest green, granite. When colors are transplanted to another climate, they don't look the same. Your place in the world has its own indigenous colors, its own light.

NEW ENGLAND
Bright white, black, navy, and red.

SOUTHWEST
Terra-cotta, blue, sage, and white.

"Pink is the navy blue of India."

DIANA VREELAND

Local Light. Picture this: You are in a room with a high ceiling and a single arched window. The floor, walls, and ceiling are painted the exact same shade of blue. Intellectually, you know that they are all the same color. But it's late afternoon and the setting sun is throwing long stripes of light across the floor. The color of the floor where the light hits now appears different from the ceiling, in deep shadow, and the far wall glows with reflection. Color is never, never static. The position of the sun or a passing cloud will change a color minute by minute. And when the sun sets and we turn the lights on, color changes again.

In daylight, yellow is the color we see best; at twilight, blue-green becomes the brightest color; at nightfall, orange and red appear darker than either green or blue.

In rooms where daylight hours are spent, use warm colors on walls that receive northern light, cool colors for southern exposures, and neutral colors on walls that greet eastern and western light.

At night, an incandescent bulb will make a yellow or cream-colored wall glow, but may turn blue and lavender walls to gray.

POWER OF PAINT

Paint has been called "canned magic." It can flatten glare in an operating room, make kindergartners want to play and color, cause a cramped little room to feel like a soothing cocoon. Paint can also raise ceilings, lengthen walls, make rooms feel more spacious or cozier, and cause design flaws to disappear in a blaze or a whisper of color.

"A painter should not paint what he sees, but what will be seen."

PAUL VALÉRY

Color as Symbol.

What's in a color? Many would find a black room mournful, even depressing. But to the Masai warrior, black is a positive color, symbolizing rain clouds in an arid land. White, the most popular paint color in the U.S., is a color of death and mourning in many Asian cultures. Red is racy: danger, sex, and "stop" implied in a single flash of crimson. Yet, oceans away, red is synonymous with happiness, purity, protection from evil. The chromopath uses blue to treat nausea and fatigue; to the astrologist, purple is the color of Sagittarius' ruling planet; and no American male would ever mistake that pink door for a men's room. Listen: Color is speaking.

INFANT
*Baby blue, powder pink,
butter yellow, and warm
white.*

CITRUS
*Lemon, lime, pale orange,
and orange.*

"I had been totally intimidated because Albers taught that one color was supposed to make the next color look better, but my feeling was that each color was itself."

ROBERT RAUSCHENBERG

The Language of Color. It is said that the human brain can perceive seven million different colors, an estimate that prompted the great colorist Josef Albers to note that "the nomenclature of color is most inadequate.... There are only about thirty color names." Apparently Professor Albers never had to choose a color for his living-room walls. Because when it comes to commercial paints, the "nomenclature of colors" is vast and baffling: thousands of paint colors with poetic names seduce us, drive us mad with possibilities, but leave us uninformed.

COLOR BASICS

COOL: *Colors that are more blue than red, and appear to recede.* **WARM:** *Colors that are more red than blue, and appear to advance. Black and white are considered neutral, but in their pure forms white is cool and black is warm.*
COMPLEMENTARY: *Colors that are opposite in the spectrum and appear to vibrate when placed next to one another. Green is the opposite of red, therefore its complement; orange is the complement of blue; violet is the complement of yellow.*
VALUE: *The lightness or darkness of a color. White has the highest value, black the lowest.* **EARTH TONES:** *Made from earth pigments such as sienna and umber. Usually brownish in color, earth tones do not appear on the color wheel.*

Paint-Chip Liberation. The long leap from idea to reality has always hindered choosing a paint color, since decisions were based on a tiny patch of color on a sample card. Now there's a crazy machine called a spectrophotometer. We can visit a paint store with a sample of anything, and this electronic wonder can scan it and come up with a paint formula to match. At Sun Wallpaper and Paint in Poughkeepsie, New York, they have scanned Formica, a green dress—while the customer was still wearing it—and an eggplant. Thanks to the spectrophotometer, your kitchen can be the color of butter, now that the world is our swatch book.

NATURE
"Our primary inspiration is nature—specifically the sensations of luminosity that are produced by the interaction of light, particulate matter in the atmosphere, and the stuff of the landscape: ground, water, trees, rocks."

DONALD KAUFMAN

"Color should reinforce the architecture,
balance the natural conditions and nurture the
soul of the inhabitants."

JOHN F. SALADINO

Planning a Paint Scheme. First, visualize. Buy fabric, matte board, wrapping paper, lettuce leaves—anything that will help you see color in volume—and tack it to your walls. Or, make simple line drawings of your rooms, have them photocopied, then experiment with watercolors, markers, colored pencil, collage. Think holistically: A progressive paint scheme is one that tells a visual story from room to room. Example: A sienna-painted foyer might lead to a warm, creamy hallway, which in turn might open onto an earthy yellow living room. That living room's light will blaze in contrast to the other two rooms. It will feel like a destination, yet all three colors will relate. The most successful paint jobs are those that consider proportion. Dark, strong colors tend to "weigh" more than pale neutrals. Say you're in love with twilight purple. In large doses, that color may overwhelm a room. Ecru-colored walls and a twilight-purple ceiling may keep your room in perfect balance while satisfying your lust for color.

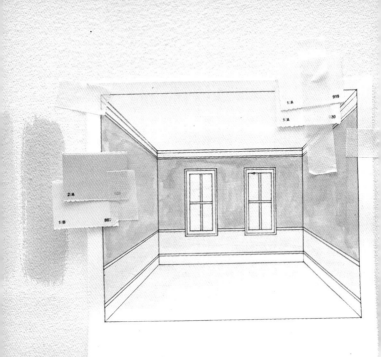

This warm-toned ceiling is drawn down toward the eye while the cool, dark walls appear to recede. Although predominantly blue, the room is cozy: the length of the windows is diminished by a chair railing. The horizontal band of blue below the chair rail "hugs" the room and emphasizes its width, rather than its height.

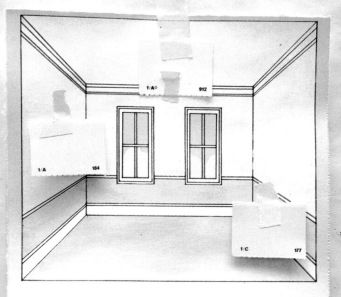

Same room, higher ceilings—or so it seems. Here, the eye is drawn to the band of color closest to the floor. Architectural boundaries are underplayed. Three tints of a single color are used; they are arranged in a progression from dark to light, so that the ceiling seems to dissolve into a bright, atmospheric haze.

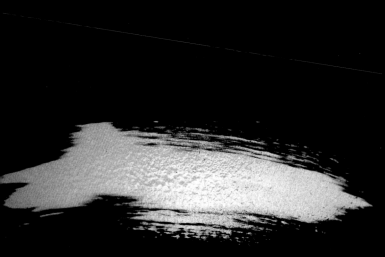

"It was the whiteness of the whale that appalled
me...there yet lurks an elusive something
in the innermost idea of this hue, which strikes
more of panic to the soul than that redness
which affrights in blood."

HERMAN MELVILLE, *Moby Dick*

White as Choice. White should always be chosen. Too many otherwise witty and imaginative citizens choose white by default. Some are victims of cultural habit. Others are simply afraid of making a mistake. Remember: White is a color of infinite tone, nuance, emotion, and power. Native Alaskan people have seventeen different words for it; Benjamin Moore has more than 200. If you choose white, choose it well.

RALPH LAUREN: *There are many whites, and they change with the day, with the sun, and with age. White can be very cool, but it can also be warm and cozy.... In my own life and in my home, white is everywhere. I wanted a place that would give me the feeling of floating. I wanted to come home and feel simplicity and peace.* CHARLES GWATHMEY: *I often select linen-white walls and white ceilings [Benjamin Moore]. In what I prefer to call holistic, integrated, and volumetric interiors, the subtle dynamics between the ceiling [horizontal] and wall [vertical] planes are reinforced and articulated, while remaining unified by the two above-mentioned whites.* MARK HAMPTON: *Benjamin Moore 918, 925, 970, and 968 are some of my favorite whites and off-whites. I use these in bedrooms and living spaces as these whites are so neutral in feeling and easy to live with.*

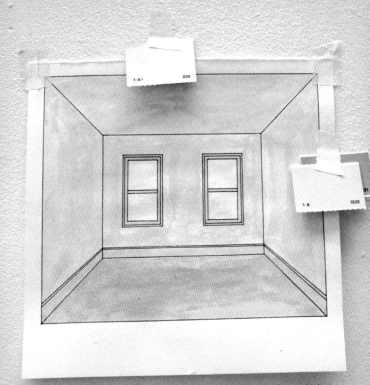

A warm-toned wood floor provides the inspiration for this palette, which gives a cozy look to an otherwise unremarkable room. Gray-green trim on the baseboards and window sash has a warming effect on the pale putty walls. The cool hue of the ceiling is atmospheric and adds height.

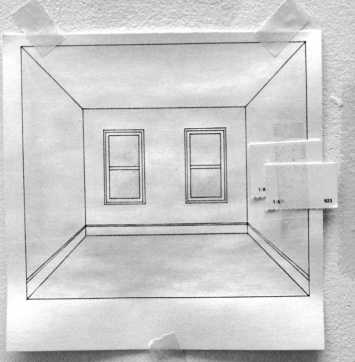

At first glance, it seems that neutral paint colors allow the scene outside the windows to become this room's focus. But a sleight of hand is at play: the warm, luminous quality of these colors gives the impression that the room is flooded with light, and the eye naturally moves toward its presumed source—the windows.

BLUEBERRY

*undiluted latex flat
by Sapolin Paint*

*Blueberry
+ black = shade*

*Blueberry
+ white = tint*

*Blueberry
+ clear = wash*

Tones. You never, ever have to use paint right out of a can. You can season your colors to taste. Too dark, add white and create a tint; too intense, make a wash by adding plain water (latex paints only). If a color lacks depth, gradually add black to create a soulful shade. When you create your own tints, shades, and washes, your colors will be related because they share the same base color. Don't be afraid; spice it up.

EVENING
Midnight blue
indigo
navy
violet blue
black

INTERIOR WISDOM

Vertically-striped walls make ceilings seem lofty. Stripes can be done freehand or by masking off areas marked with a plumb line. Yellow is perceived by the eye as radiant, and can make a dark space brighter. Shades of pink that seem subtle on a paint chip can end up looking like Pepto-Bismol. Choose a neutral shade with only a hint of pink. Avoid using white or high-value colors on floors. Because the eye tends to cast downward, a too-bright floor can cause a kind of snow blindness—that is, everything else in the room will look tiny and isolated.

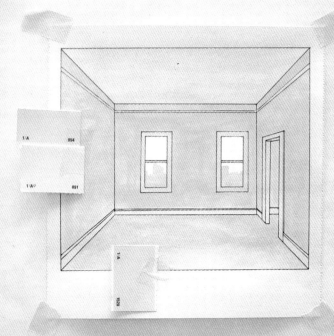

By painting a room in a single, distinctive color, architectural flaws can be
disguised and diminished. Here, pale green walls are accompanied by trim in a
very-slightly-lighter tint. The distinct color forces your eye to move around the
room and not rest on any one detail, so flaws flatten away.

Five historic colors enliven this formal entryway. The ornate doorway is framed by a brick-red wall, its shape further highlighted by the complementary colors in the hallway. The slate-gray baseboard trim acts as a grounding device for the strong color contrasts.

The Colors of Aging. The world looks different to a 70-year-old than it does to a 20-year-old. Besides the inner vision that comes with wisdom and experience, there is the physiological matter of the eye itself. With age, the lens of the eye tends to yellow. This affects "color vision" and can make certain colors difficult to distinguish. Choosing appropriate colors for an older person's home is crucial, since it has been found that poor color vision contributes to incidences of falling in the home.

COLOR AID

1. *For a person with poor color vision, the most difficult colors to distinguish between are pure blues and greens; pale tints of different colors with the same intensities, such as baby pink and baby blue; and dark tones of different colors with the same intensities, such as midnight blue and plum.* 2. *Rooms with highly-contrasting colors are the safest. One recommended color scheme: paint walls a solid, medium-toned blue; paint trim and furniture with bright, warm colors such as red, orange, and yellow.* 3. *To help signal a change in elevation between adjacent rooms, paint floors in strongly contrasting colors. If floors are on the same level, use the same or similar intensities of floor colors, making sure that floors are contrasted with walls in all cases.*

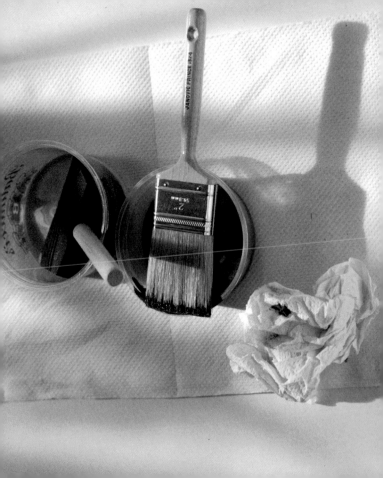

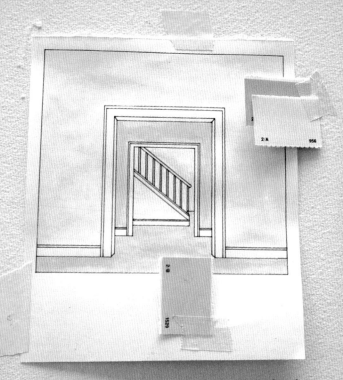

*Variations on a theme: three neutral shades move the eye through a
triple entrance. There is an illusion of increased depth because the cool, putty
color on the stairway appears to recede. The white trim serves as a
visual connector between the three areas.*

Here, warm colors brighten and foreshorten the passageway. Architectural details are articulated by the strong red in the center room. Because the colors are all in the same family, the overall effect is cheerful but not garish. The color pulls both your eye and yourself from room to room.

A P P L I C A T I O N

You're dying to cover that wall. You want to bathe it in paint, to immerse it smoothly and completely like the globe on a Sherwin Williams logo. But you can't, not yet, because incompatible surfaces can cause a war of the walls. Before you even look at a brush, your ceilings and walls and floors must be properly prepared. All paints are fussy about where they're spread. If a wall is dirty, dusty, greasy, glossy, or crumbly, even the best paint will eventually peel off, dropping unsightly chips into your guests' martinis.

> "What I wanted to do was paint sunlight on the side of a house."

EDWARD HOPPER

Prep Tools

NOTCHED TROWEL

FIVE-IN-ONE TOOL

TAPING KN

PAINT SCRAPER

DROP CLOTH

ONE-INCH PUTTY KNIFE

SPACKLE

TAPE

BROAD TAPING KNIFE

DISPOSABLE DUST MASK

SANDPAPER

"It is perseverance
that makes the difference
between seduction
and courtship."

THE I CHING

Prep 101. VACUUM or dust surfaces. With an ammonia/water solution, SCRUB splatters, scuffs, and crayon marks from walls and ceilings. COVER grease and water stains with a commercial stain sealer. SAND glossy surfaces to a dull texture, or scrub with an abrasive cleanser like Comet. Thoroughly rinse and dry. With a scraper, FLATTEN peeling paint, bubbles, and loose plaster. Undercut small cracks and holes with a putty knife, then PACK with spackle, joint compound, or toothpaste (not the kind with stripes or sparkles). Smooth to a flat surface; sand when dry. DUST, then prime the repaired areas. When dry, PRIME entire wall. Now you can start to PAINT.

PRIMER PRIMER

1. *Use primer if you plan to paint a light color over a dark color.* 2. *Prime all raw, never-before-painted surfaces.* 3. *If you want to turn a light wall into a dark one, add a colorant to your primer. Colorants are available in tubes and can save you extra coats of expensive finish paint.* 4. *A good primer can seep under flaking paint and help glue it down.* 5. *Beware of "all-purpose" primers. Buy a primer that's specifically designed for the surface area of the job at hand.*

Prepping the Problem Surface. Take heart: with information and elbow grease, any wall can be repaired and repainted.

SKIM-COATING Damaged plaster or Sheetrock surfaces, sand-painted ceilings, or stuck wallpaper can be skim-coated. Repair holes with spackle, then cover entire wall with a thin, smooth coat of joint compound. Sand rough areas, then dust and paint.

CANVASING Crumbling walls can be entirely covered with canvas. Apply with wallpaper paste, then skim-coat, sand smooth, and prime.

WALLPAPERED SURFACES Pull on a corner of the wallpaper. If it peels away, remove it all, then sand and prime the wall. If it's stuck, glue down loose spots, scrape off peeling edges, feather in bare areas with spackle. Then sand, dust, and seal with an oil-based primer. **WOOD-PANELED SURFACES** Wash with an industrial-strength detergent or an abrasive cleanser. Rinse and let dry, then sand, and apply an oil-based primer. When dry, sand again, dust, and cover with an oil-based paint.

ROLLER WITH LAMB'S-WOOL
COVER FOR OIL-BASED PAINT

MIXING STICKS

OVAL SASH BRUSH

TWO-INCH ANGULAR
SASH BRUSH,
SYNTHETIC

CHISEL-END
BRUSH, TWO-
INCH,
NATURAL

MASKING TAPE

PAPER TAPE

NATURAL SEA SPONGE

ER TRAY

SAFETY
GOGGLES

FOUR-INCH BRUSHES, FLAT END

DISPOSABLE GLOVES

"To have begun is half the job:
be bold and be sensible."

HORACE

Like a Pro. Always work from top to bottom. Wear a hat. When working with a roller use long, back-and-forth movements in a "W" pattern, making sure each stroke smoothes the edges of the one before it. If surfaces look spotty at first, don't fret: Latex paint dries in patches but eventually evens out. Oil-based paint should be applied with a brush. Paint in a crisscross pattern, then use a light, upward stroke to smooth out brush marks. When painting trim, dip only the tip of your brush into the paint and use long strokes in one direction. Avoid painting yourself or your telephone into a corner.

BEFORE YOU START

1. *Remove switch plates, outlet plates, hardware, and doorknobs.* 2. *Mask off built-in fixtures.* 3. *Set up strong secondary lighting.* 4. *Cover floors and furniture with drop cloths.* 5. *With a mixing stick, stir your paint in a figure-eight pattern.* 6. *When you're sure that no sediment is settled on the bottom, decant a workable amount of paint into a lightweight bucket and re-seal the can.*

How To. **CEILINGS** Start at the window end of a room and work away from the light. With a two-inch brush, paint the ceiling where it meets the walls and trim. Latex painters may then use a roller fitted with an extension; oil-based paint requires a brush of not more than four inches. **WALLS** Work in horizontal bands from the ceiling downward. **TRIM** Paint crown molding, windows, chair rails, doors, and baseboards, in that order. **WINDOWS** Raise the lower sash as high as it will go and lower the upper sash halfway. Start with inner frames, placing a trim guard against the glass, then move on to sashes and sills. Leave the window open a few inches to prevent sticking. If you get paint on the glass, wait until it sets before scraping with a razor blade. **DOORS** Follow the "inside-out" rule; for panel areas, apply paint in one direction and feather it out in the opposite direction. **FLOORS** Paint by hand, beginning with a two-inch brush in the corners and then finishing with a wide brush.

Quality. Buy high-quality paint. The price of cheap paint can be alluring, but it will cost you more in the long run. Paint is essentially composed of three elements: pigment, which gives paint its color; binder, which carries the pigment and dries to a protective film; and diluent, which thins paint. Of the three elements, pigment is the most expensive. Manufacturers of "bargain" paints substitute "pigment extenders" (i.e., cheap fillers) to thicken their paints. More filler equals less pigment; less pigment equals poor coverage; poor coverage equals more coats of paint. A high-quality paint requires less product to get the job done and lasts longer.

"Some people, including some people who work in paint stores...believe that latex paint is for amateurs and sissies—the light beer of paint."

DAVID OWEN,
The Walls Around Us

SPRING
Light blue-green, natural whites and grays

1. Ground aluminum

2. Copper

3. Iron powder

4. Indigo

5. Cochineal

6. Madder lake

7. Red jasper

8. Malachite

9. Lapis lazuli

10. Italian siena

11. German umber

12. French ochre

Mica, flaked & whole

Marble, Alpengrün,
Verona white, crushed,
marble dust

Sanguine, soft red chalk

Pumice stone,
whole &
powdered

Chalk from Bologna

Dralon fiber

Latex Paints. Most commercial water-based paints are latex, made from tiny plastic particles suspended in water. As it dries, it leaves behind a mesh of particles and pigment. Latex paints look best in flat finishes because latex itself is naturally flat; manufacturers must force it to become glossy by manipulating the latex particles.

Oil-based Paints. Once oil paints were composed of pigments and linseed oil. Today, "oil-based paint" is really "alkyd-based paint": a polyester dissolved in a petroleum-based solvent. When alkyd paint dries it combines with oxygen molecules in the air. The results: a watertight, hardened resin.

LATEX PAINT, PRO & CON:
Quick to apply, quick to dry, but can remain tacky even when set. Ecologically kinder than oil paint, but tends to soften when moist. Virtually odorless, but lacks depth. Successful in flat finishes, but gloss finishes can look like plastic.

OIL PAINT, PRO & CON:
Chemically binds to surfaces, but smells like petrochemicals. Dries to a hard surface, but slowly. Has great depth, but requires clean-up with toxic, flammable liquids. Excellent for gloss finishes, but matte finishes are not as flat as latex-based.

Paint Finishes.

FLAT OR MATTE A non-reflective finish suited to walls that are in less-than-perfect condition. **EGGSHELL** Slightly more lustrous than flat paint, with a subtle texture that makes it ideal for semi-stressed walls. **PEARL** A slightly luminous paint that resembles a laminate surface when dry. **LOW-LUSTRE OR SATIN** A soft, warm finish traditionally used for woodwork and trim. **SEMI-GLOSS** Somewhat shiny and infinitely washable. Good for fingerprint-prone areas such as door frames, window sash, and kitchen and bathroom walls. **HIGH-GLOSS** A reflective and durable finish most successful in oil-based formulas. Good for high traffic areas; accentuates surface blemishes.

PAINT MYSTERIES SOLVED

"Enamel" refers to paints that dry to a hard, washable surface. The term is confusing because enamel paints were originally a high-gloss, lacquer-based coating. Now, enamel paints can be alkyd or latex, and are available in all finishes, including flat. Areas that are exposed to moisture such as bathroom walls, windowsills, and kitchen cabinets fare best with oil-based paints in enamel formulas. Flat paints tend to dry lighter than the color on the label, while gloss and semi-gloss paints tend to dry darker.

Benjamin Moore & Co., Regal Wall
Satin Latex Interior Flat, #1407

Benjamin Moore & Co., Impervex
Latex High-Gloss Enamel, #1407

Texture. From the crumbling walls of an abandoned convent to the sparkling swirls on your grandmother's stuccoed ceiling, texture captures light and plays with it. Clapboard, cracked plaster, worm-holed woodwork, stone: Paint can approximate the patina of age, can texture a wall in infinite ways. With a sanding block, attack a wall and watch it become rough and whitened. Rub it deeply and witness *pentimento*— the sudden surfacing of layers of paint that have lurked beneath the surface for years. Take artificial leaves, paste them up, and paint right over them. Add sand, glitter, or kitty litter to your paint. Or thin it and apply it with a stiff brush: spatter it, stipple it, sponge it, rub it, rough it up.

"As every decorator knows, flat, uniform colour is inert and unyielding, while distressed or broken colour is suggestive, atmospheric. Walls treated with distressed paint are volatilized, the bare facts of bricks and mortar dissolved in a fluent movement of transparent colour shadows and highlights. The plainest box of a room, built yesterday, can be transformed with the right distressed paint finish into a place with soul."

JOCASTA INNES,
The New Paint Magic

Brushes. Colors come and go, but a good paintbrush, if treated with kind intelligence, will last a lifetime. Maybe two. Oil-based painting requires brushes made of natural bristles—usually Chinese hog bristles—which swell when loaded with paint. Latex painting calls for synthetic-bristle brushes, which are typically made from polyester. Like the paints to which they are dedicated, natural and synthetic brushes don't mix. If a natural brush is used in a latex paint, it will soak up the water, dry out the paint, and injure the brush. An even more disastrous mix is synthetic brushes and oil-based paints: Some synthetic fibers, especially nylon, will dissolve in certain oil-compatible solvents.

BRUSH KNOW-HOW

Most paint jobs require two or three different brushes: **1.** *A two-inch, angular sash brush for windows and trim.* **2.** *A three-inch, chisel-end brush for larger areas of fine brush work, such as doors.* **3.** *A four-inch, flat-end brush for expansive surfaces.* **4.** *Good brushes have bristles of varying lengths that have split ends.* **5.** *Check brushes for gaps (a sign of a cheap brush); be sure only a few bristles shed.* **6.** *Check for flex. When bent, it should spring back into shape.* **7.** *Beware of China or ox-hair "blends." They may contain only a small percentage of quality bristles.*

ARTIST'S CUTTER BRUSH

FOUR INCH CHISEL-END
WALL BRUSH

ONE-
HALF
AN
SASH

THREE-INCH
FLAT-END
WALL BRUSH

LONG-HANDLED
ONE-INCH SASH
BRUSH

OVAL SASH AND TRIM
BRUSH, FOR USE WITH
GLOSS FORMULAS

OVAL SASH AND TRIM
BRUSH

TWO-INCH
ANGULAR SASH
BRUSH

Colorwashing. Do you want walls the color of iced tea or swimming-pool water? Experts will tell you that these colors take their beauty not from pigment but from light. Common house paints use white to approximate light, but adding white to any pure color is like adding milk to iced tea: that shimmering liquid becomes opaque. Although walls can't become sources of light, a similar effect can be managed by thinning latex paint with water and brushing it on in layers —a technique known as colorwashing. Apply colorwash in expressive strokes on a primed wall, allowing layers to dry between coats.

GLAZE IT

Glazed walls have infinite depth and shine, and are created with a mixture of commercial oil glaze, paint thinner, linseed oil, and oil-based paints. Apply it in thin layers and allow it to dry between coats. For a smooth, glass-like finish, apply glazes with a soft, round-edged brush.

"Make a choice that puts you at home in the world, that expresses your particular place, your self. Don't be afraid to try, don't be afraid to fail. How many chances do you have to control your environment? Quit beating around the bush and put it on the goddamn wall."

ALEXANDER
JULIAN

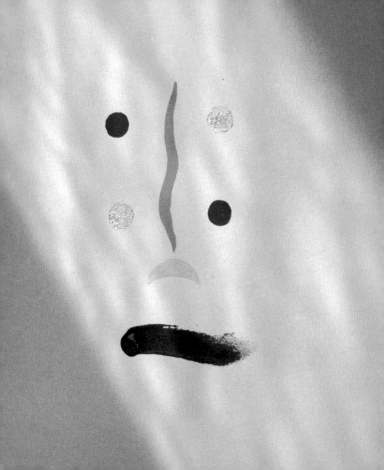

palettes.

Follow "palette" to its root and you will find the Latin "pala," meaning "spade." To artists, a palette is both the board on which colors are mixed and the range of colors within a composition. Every individual has his or her own personal palette: It is simply that unique collection of colors with which each of us chooses to surround ourselves.

NEO-CLASSICAL
Black, gold, white

COLOR BASICS

Primary colors: Pure red, yellow, and blue.
Secondary colors: Orange, green, violet, made by mixing primary colors.
Related colors: Colors that have a common primary in their mixture. Violet, teal, and lavender can be considered related if they're all made with the same shade of blue.
Monochromatic: Color schemes that use tints, tones, and shades of the same base color.
Analogous: Color schemes that use related colors.

"All the paints in the Donald Kaufman Color Collection have overtones. Being formulated with as many as 13 pigments from across the entire spectrum, each color has the ability to go in more than one direction, to shift with the light and the colors in the vicinity and work with greater flexibility than ordinary paint colors. Color #26, which we call Tea Green, has found wide acceptance for a variety of rooms: living, dining, studies, halls. It's warm enough for comfort, green enough to evoke nature, gray enough to remain neutral and avoid an obvious reading, and blue enough to perform as cool and shadowy."
Donald Kaufman, interview

COLOR PARTNERS

Hardwood floors/woodwork: Try neutral colors: cream, ivory, ecru, to integrate the wood's color for a natural look. For a balanced feeling, create a complementary scheme with cool, dark colors such as teal or forest green.

Exposed brick: To highlight brick, use a contrasting blue or blue-green color that has a touch of red in its mix. To downplay a brick wall, choose colors which can be found in the brick itself: pinkish terracotta, reddish umber, or off-white to match the mortar.

"My house here is painted the yellow color of fresh butter on the outside with glaringly green shutters...It is completely whitewashed inside, and the floor is made of red tiles. And over it there is the intensely blue sky. In this I can live and breathe, meditate, and paint."
VINCENT VAN GOGH

VAN GOGH COLORS
Blue, gold, orange, brown, green, gray, rust

Marble/stone: Marble or stone fireplaces become the focus of a room when surrounded by strong colors. Complement ivory-toned stone with an eggshell paint in ruby, ochre, or olive green; to highlight rough gray stone try warm tones: burgundy, deep raspberry, lavender-tinted gray.

White porcelain: Sinks, tubs, and tiles of bright white may seem neutral, but in fact the shine of porcelain needs highly-saturated red, yellows, or aquamarines to match its intensity. If you prefer subtle tints, use high-gloss paint.

COLOR SYMBOLISM

COLORS OF THE RULING PLANETS

Sun (Leo): Gold, bright yellow, red, yellow-green

Moon (Cancer): Silver, white, emerald green, dark green, smoky gray

Mars (Aries): Red, crimson, scarlet, white

Venus (Libra, Taurus): Blue, blue-green, turquoise

Mercury (Gemini, Virgo): Yellow, orange, lilac, off-white

Jupiter (Sagittarius): Purple, violet, russet red

Saturn (Capricorn): Olive green, gray, dark green, black

Uranus (Aquarius): Electric blue, pale green, citrine

Neptune (Pisces): Dark blue, indigo, gray, green, pink, coral

Pluto (Scorpio): Yellow, pale green, navy

Earth: Lavender, blue, white

COLORS OF THE CHROMOPATH

Blue: Heals wounds, inflammation, burns, headache, fatigue, hysteria, convulsion, apoplexy, epilepsy, heart palpitation, pleurisy, gastritis, nausea, indigestion, diarrhea, toothache.

Red: Stimulates circulation. Used to treat depression, anemia, masculine impotency, "feminine apathy," and "those cursed with a repugnance for humanity."

Yellow: Stimulates mental powers, circulates energy; used to treat memory loss, heartburn, sluggish liver, constipation, tuberculosis, hearing loss.

Green: Used to calm the digestive organs and, along with violet and ruby, as a treatment for cancer.

Orange: Used to treat baldness and colic.

Violet: Prescribed for insomnia.

PERSONAL PALETTE

"I prefer vibrant color in small doses, like ruby red lipstick with khakis and a white shirt. Or intense flowers in a very neutral room. Nature has a lovely way of putting color where it belongs."

Eve Ashcraft, color and paint consultant

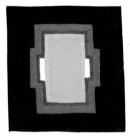

ORGANIC
Gold, rust, black

FRANK LLOYD WRIGHT
Teal, sandalwood, cream, green

"Of the colors, blue and green have the greatest emotional range. Sad reds and melancholy yellows are difficult to turn up.... Although green enlivens the earth and mixes in the ocean, and we find it, copperish, in fire; green air, green skies are rare. Gray and brown are widely distributed, but there are no joyful swatches of either, or any of exuberant black, sullen pink, or acquiescent orange. Blue is therefore most suitable as the color of interior life."

WILLIAM GASS,
On Being Blue

first aid.

Paint consumers have to be artists, contractors, and chemistry majors, all in one. For whichever hat, here are some helpful tips.

CHEMISTRY

OIL PAINT: NOT GREEN

For all the years you can remember, oil-based paint has been polluting your living room. For each gallon that dried, roughly half a gallon of petrochemical solvent evaporated into the atmosphere. Every time a brush was cleaned with paint thinner, more toxins entered into the world. Laws limiting VOCs, or volatile organic compounds, have been passed and enacted. As a result, alkyd-based paints with fewer solvents are being introduced, and new formulas are being devised that tread more gently on the earth.

BETTER LIVING THROUGH SCIENCE

For a few bad years back in the '80s, ecologically-correct paints were a consumer's nightmare. Some turned yellow, others covered poorly. But technology has quickly caught up with the law. According to Simon Rosenblum, paint expert at Janovic/Plaza, New York, new acrylic formulas are outperforming traditional oil-based paints. Even in kitchens and bathrooms, says Rosenblum, acrylic paints are durable, trouble-free, and aesthetically appealing.

DON'T BUY IT

Latex paints have always been within recommended VOC thresholds. If you see a can of latex with an inflated price tag and a label that brags, "Conforms to VOC standards for the year 2000," just chuckle.

P.C. PAINT

Eco Design Co., based in New Mexico, manufactures and imports paints made with non-toxic mineral pigments, no heavy metals, and no synthetics. Ingredients include flax, tree resins, tung oil, and sugar beet alcohol. The paints are a blessing to chemically-sensitive people who can't tolerate the toxins found in conventional paints.

White lead is a poisonous pigment which, when ingested or inhaled, stays in the body and can injure organs and brain cells. Though limited by law since 1978, some 40 million homes in the U.S. have lead paint in them, usually on metal surfaces (pipes, radiators) and on high-traffic areas (stairs, doors, windows). Old paint tends to chip and children are attracted to the colorful pieces. But a more dangerous fact is this: certain formulas of lead paint were designed to "chalk" when exposed to sunlight, creating a fine powdery dust which, when washed away, left a bright, new-looking surface. In lead paint, that "chalk" is pure lead carbonate—almost irresistible for a kid to touch, and ultimately ingest.

LEAD ABATEMENT

You can have your home tested for lead, and hire a professional who specializes in lead abatement, but be warned: There is no truly safe way to remove lead paint. If you're home alone with lead, do not sand or scrape it. Sanding creates lead-filled dust that can settle in food, furniture, and lungs. Likewise, avoid chemical paint strippers—they create lead-heavy goop that, in turn, has to be removed. Do paint over it. Sealing it under new paint will prevent loved ones from breathing or eating lead carbonates and residues.

"Removing decay, scraping away various foreign accumulations, applying filling material—these dentistry-evocative activities are among my favorite home-improvement chores. Equally as satisfying, I suppose, are the ways in which repairing plaster does not resemble dentistry: the tools are large, the work is not done inside people's mouths, walls don't have breath."

DAVID OWEN,
The Walls Around Us

MERCURY & LATEX: YET ANOTHER THING TO WORRY ABOUT

You've found some old cans of latex in the basement. You figure you'll thin 'em down, add some tints, and give 'em a whirl on your walls. Watch out: You may be filling your house with dangerous mercury vapors, which can hang around for a year or more. Up until 1990, when it was banned by the EPA, mercury was used as an additive in approximately 30 percent of interior latex paints as a bacteria and mold killer.

BEAUTIFUL POISON

In the interest of preservation, historical accuracy, or just plain old-fashioned beauty, we may travel to the ends of the earth (or just Europe) for the perfect pigment. But be warned: many pigments are highly toxic when inhaled or swallowed and must be handled with extreme care. They are: Zinc White, Zinc Yellow, Lead White, Lead Minum, Chrome Yellow, Chrome Orange, Chrome Green, Molybdenum, Massicot, Naples Yellow, Ground Glass, Lithopone, Blanc Fix, Manganese Blue, all Cobalt Blues, Cobalt Violet, Cobalt Green, Cobalt Yellow, Smalt, Heliogen Blue, Heliogen Green, Malachite, Azurite, Verdigris, Mountain Blue, Vermilion, Nickeltitanium Yellow, Indian Yellow, and all Cadmium pigments, which become toxic when burned.

PAINT BOX

HOW MUCH SHOULD YOU BUY?

Most paint labels inform consumers that a gallon of paint will cover a 400- to 450-square-foot surface. Those figures are misleading because they're based on the thickest possible application. In the real world, do-it-yourselfers apply paint in fairly thin coats. It's therefore smarter to estimate that a gallon of paint yields 600 to 650 square feet of coverage.

HOW TO ESTIMATE LIKE A PRO

Painting contractors, before estimating a job, have to think of everything. Since they charge anywhere from $30 to $45 an hour and have to displace their customers for the duration of the job, they'd better think of everything. Do-it-yourselfers, no matter how impulsive, should consider the very same factors:

*1. **Paint quality/expense.** A gallon of paint covers approximately 600 square feet of flat wall, and most jobs require two to four coats.*

*2. **Prep time.** Besides reserving time for scraping and scrubbing, add time for moving furniture, masking off fixtures, and draping the world with drop cloths.*

*3. **Painting time.** Rollers are quicker than brushes; walls are quicker than ceilings; painting trim is the slowest of all; and everything is going to require at least two coats.*

4. Drying time. *Paint must be allowed to dry not only between coats but between colors. Remember: oil paint takes much longer to dry than latex.*

5. Clean-up time. *Consider the brush-washing, the roller-rinsing, the tarp-folding, the furniture-moving and—oh yes—the window-scraping.*

HOW LONG WILL IT LAST

The shinier the paint, the easier it is to wash. A dappled wall can be created by adding dashes of warm and cool colorants (artists' acrylics will work just fine), and shine can be had with the addition of acrylic gloss medium.

SPECIALTY PAINTS

Deck paint: *Has a thick consistency and dries to a hard shine. Originally developed for marine use, it's preferred for floors because of its durability.*

Casein paint: *Essentially a dairy product, casein is made from the dried curd of skim milk. It has long been used to paint theatrical scenery because of its flat, non-reflective finish. Although it has a reputation of being unwashable and prone to spoiling, modern commercial casein is durable and ideal for chemically-sensitive folk.*

Buttermilk paint: *Pure buttermilk was once used by artists to flatten too-glossy surfaces on oil paintings. Buttermilk paint, a cousin of casein, was used by Shakers for decorative*

work and is still available in specialty stores— generally in small quantities.

Plant color glaze: *A line of bright color concentrates for natural-looking glaze techniques. Manufactured by Livos, a German plant chemistry company, ingredients have low toxicity and include extract of plant color, clay binder, beeswax, and orange peel oil.*

Egg tempera: *An ancient paint that can be made at home using egg yolks and powdered pigments. Time-consuming, permanent, and lovely for hand-painted wall designs.*

Metallic paint: *Real gold leafing involves paper-thin sheets of hammered gold that must be burnished to surfaces. Metallic paints can approximate the look of gold leaf, and are available in copper, silver, and bronze as well as gold, or try bronzing powders mixed with oil or shellac. For best results, start with an ochre-colored base coat and finish with two or more coats of metallic paint.*

TOOLS OF THE TRADE

BRUSHES VS. ROLLERS

Whether you brush or roll depends on what kind of paint you choose. Rollers work best with latex paint and aren't advised for use with slow-drying oil-based paints, as the roller tends to leave visible marks. When working with high-gloss paint in any formula, avoid rollers altogether.

THE CARE AND FEEDING OF FINE BRUSHES

It's worth spending good money on good brushes. If you treat them right, they'll outlive dozens of paint jobs. Here's how:

- *Before using a new brush, wash it in warm water and soap and tease out any loose bristles.*

- *How to wash a brush: Rinse it in warm (not hot) water, then swirl it against a bar of Murphy's Oil Soap until the bristles are foamy right up to the heel (the part nearest the handle). Rinse and flex until the water runs clear, then press excess water out of the bristles.*

- *To clean oil-based paint from your brush, fill two containers with paint thinner. Dip and swirl the brush in the first container, then squeeze excess pigment from the bristles with your gloved hands. Swirl the brush again in the second, cleaner container. Squeegee the brush by hand, then wash it as described above.*

- *If you don't have time to clean your brushes at the end of the day, tape them to the inside of a container of paint thinner or water (depending on what kind of paint you've been using). Make sure the bristles are immersed in solvent but not resting on the container's bottom.*

- *See that hole in your brush's handle? Hang it on a hook for drying and storage.*

SHOPPING TIPS

- *Quality brushes have a lot of bristles of varying lengths.*

- *A good brush has bristles that are "flagged"; that is, they have split ends. Flagged bristles hold more paint at the tip and yield a finer brush stroke.*

- *Before buying a brush, spread out the bristles to check for gaps (a sign of a cheap brush) and to see how many bristles the brush sheds. A few shed bristles is normal, but more than three may indicate that bristles are improperly embedded in the heel.*

- *Check for flex. A good brush will bend more at its tip than at its base and will quickly spring back to its original shape.*

- *Beware of China or ox-hair "blends." They may be cheap brushes with only a small percent of high-quality bristles.*

SPECIALTY BRUSHES

Foam brush: *Designed to be discarded after use; good for touch-ups or for testing colors.*

Radiator brush: *Long-handled sash brush, bent at a 45-degree angle, for painting radiators and the walls behind them.*

Oval sash brush: *An oval-headed brush which gives a particularly smooth finish to high-gloss or enamel paint.*

Dragging brush: *For dragging and graining techniques; has thick nylon bristles on one side and natural hair on the other.*

Stencil brush: *Short, round, stiff brush used for stenciling.*

Stippling brush: *Short-haired brush resembling a scrub brush for stipple and spatter techniques.*

Sea sponge: *Natural sponge with irregular textures and pitted surfaces, best for decorative sponging.*

ROLLERAMA

Rollers may not offer the lifetime of service that brushes do, but they're worthy of serious study. A cheap roller can smear your paint by turning too slowly or spatter it by spinning too fast, and may fall apart—at an inconvenient moment—after a few washings.

• *Make sure the grip is comfortable in your hand and has threads for fitting an extension handle.*

• *Avoid handles that require the removal of screws in order to replace the sleeve—when clogged with paint they can be a nuisance.*

• *Synthetic sleeves are usually made from nylon and are recommended for use with latex paints. Natural roller sleeves are made of lamb's wool and are exclusively for use with oil-based paints.*

• *The rougher the surface being painted, the longer the nap on your roller should be. Shorter naps are for satin, eggshell, and high-gloss painting against a smooth surface, while the longest naps are for textured surfaces such as stucco.*

• *Avoid roller sleeves that have cardboard cores; they absorb moisture and don't hold up to washing.*

GUN CONTROL

Big jobs call for big guns. The airless spray gun, while not particularly big, is powerful. It can pump thinned paint at an approximate pressure of 3,000 pounds per square inch and as fast as 200 miles per hour. Such force can be deadly, so airless spray guns must be given the same respect as real guns.

A better argument for the use of the airless spray gun is that it's fast and flexible. High-quality models come fitted with a flexible extension tip. Ceilings, floors, and hard-to-reach areas can be covered with such easy speed that it may even justify all that extra masking.

ON THE JOB

HANDY TIP

Beauticians, lab technicians, and dental hygienists all use disposable plastic gloves, and so should you. Available by the box at hardware and beauty supply stores, they'll save your hands from chemicals, pigments, and ruined manicures.

WHAT A CATCH

When painting ceilings with a brush, make yourself a "drip-catcher" by poking the handle through an aluminum or paper plate.

THE CUTTING EDGE

You can make an angled brush even sharper by wrapping an elastic band around the bristles. This will keep it from splaying at the edges and will give you more control when painting trim.

YOU'RE SOAKING IN IT

After working with oil-based paints, try cleaning your hands (but never your brush) with a mixture of corn oil and dishwashing detergent. Though not as fast as cleaning up with paint thinner, the mixture is kind to sensitive skin.

SONGS TO PAINT A ROOM BY

"New Coat of Paint," Tom Waits
"Paint It Black," The Rolling Stones
"Black & White World," Elvis Costello
"White Room," Cream
"Blue Motel Room," Joni Mitchell
"Little Pink Houses," John Mellencamp
"Red Rain," Peter Gabriel
"Purple Rain," Prince
"Purple Haze," Jimi Hendrix
"Mellow Yellow," Donovan
"For Artists Only," Talking Heads

AFTER THE FACT

DISASTER RELIEF

Your paint job is all finished. You absolutely loathe it. Why start again from scratch? Instead, try some paint doctoring.

For too-glossy walls: *With fine sandpaper wrapped around a block, lightly rough up the surface. Use circular, sweeping arm movements on large areas and tighter, closer movements on areas that butt against edges and trim.*

For too-flat walls: *Cover surfaces with a coat of clear gloss. For latex-based paints use an acrylic gloss medium. For oil-based paints try shellac or high-gloss polyurethane (warning: both emit overpowering vapors).*

For too-dark walls: *Take approximately a quart of leftover paint and thin it with 50 percent water or solvent. Add a high-value colorant. For warm base colors try yellow or ochre; for cool base colors add white or off-white. With a large brush or rag, apply thin layers of the lighter color to the walls, allowing it to dry between coats.*

For too-bright walls: *Follow the above steps, choosing a deeper colorant such as umber (dark brown), alizarin crimson (dark maroon), ultramarine (dark blue), or sienna (warm medium brown). For a subtle toning down, try a darker tint of your base color.*

A RETURN ON YOUR INVESTMENT

Lots of stores take returns on unopened cans of paint. Even custom-mixed colors can be returned, although some stores will charge a 25 percent re-stocking fee.

WELL-DISPOSED

Check with your town or city ordinances regarding disposal of leftover paints and solvents. Often, oil-based paints, paint thinner, and turpentine must be professionally disposed of, and such services can be astronomically expensive. Although some cities have special drop-off areas at the local dump, the best thing to do with oil-based leftovers is share them or re-use them. Latex paint is less hazardous and can be legally discarded if it's allowed to dry into a solid. To speed up the process, divide unused paint into small, open containers.

THE WHITEWASH RECIPE

Ingredients:

- *1 seven-pound bag of whiting, available from hardware and paint retailers*
- *1 one-pound bag of rabbit skin glue, available at artists' supply stores*
- *Water*

Half-fill a small bucket with cold water and pour in whiting until it is about 4 inches above the surface of the water. Leave it to soak for an hour.

In the meantime, prepare rabbit skin glue by mixing it with water according to directions on the package. Stand the glue container in a pan of hot water and heat slowly until it is warm and runny.

When one hour has lapsed, stir the whiting mixture vigorously to make a smooth paste. Pour in the warmed glue and mix thoroughly. Apply immediately—the whitewash will not keep for more than a day or two. If the mixture stiffens or becomes too thick, stand the container in a large bucket of warm water.

Whitewash can be used in any consistency desired. For a milky effect, keep the whitewash as thin as skim milk; for a smooth surface without brush marks, keep it to the consistency of heavy cream.

Note: Whitewash doesn't have to be white. Before adding the glue you can tint your whiting mixture by adding spoonfuls of powdered pigment, pre-dissolved in a little cold water.

> "A hooker told me she'd do anything I wanted for fifty bucks. I said, 'Paint my house.'"
>
> HENNY YOUNGMAN

where. You can find the custom formula, the ideal brush, a voice of wisdom. Whether you seek raw pigments or polished, professional decorators, here is a world of perfect finishes waiting to be born.

FREEDOM OF CHOICE

Even as the world shrinks and chain stores expand globally, there are plenty of locales where choice is limited if there is any choice at all. However, most manufacturers today can aid you in finding a store or even mail direct to you. The U.S. numbers listed below will help give you freeedom of choice.

MANUFACTURERS

Ace	800/223-8663	Kelly-Moore	800/874-4436
Behr	800/854-0133	Pittsburgh Paints	800/441-9695
Benjamin Moore	800/826-2623	Pratt & Lambert	800/289-7728
Colony	800/845-9061	Sears	800/972-4687
Devoe	800/654-2616	Sherwin Williams	216/566-2151
Dutch Boy	800/828-5669	Standard Brands	310/214-2411
Enterprise	800/845-9061	Tru-Test	800/922-0061
Fuller O'Brien	800/368-2068	Valspar	800/845-9061
		Wards	800/695-3553

United States

CALIFORNIA

CREATIVE PAINT &
WALLPAPER
5435 Geary Boulevard
San Francisco, CA
94121-2306
415/666-3380
(Paint and decorative supplies)

DELTA/SHIVA
2550 Pellissier Place
Whittier, CA 90601
213/686-0678
(Artists' paints and supplies)

JO SONJA'S
FOLK ART, INC.
2136 Third Street
Eureka, CA 95501
707/445-9306
*(Acrylic paint, brushes, and
supplies)*

MANN BROTHERS
757 North La Brea Avenue
Hollywood, CA 90038
213/936-5168
(Paints and lacquers)

COLORADO

DIAMOND VOGEL
4500 East 48th Avenue
Denver, CO 80216
303/333-4499
(Paints)

CONNECTICUT

AMERICAN PAINT &
DECORATING
36 Welles Street
Glastonbury, CT 06033
203/633-9493
(Paint and decorating supplies)

GILBER'S PAINTS
1739 Post Road East
Westport, CT 06880
203/255-3415
(Historic colors)

LITCHFIELD PAINT &
WALLPAPER
172 West Street
Box 1118
Litchfield, CT 06759
203/567-4131
*(Paint, wallpaper, and
sundries)*

MARLBORO COUNTRY
BARN
North Main Street
Marlboro, CT 06447
203/295-8231
*(Interior and exterior paints
and supplies)*

WOODWORKERS STORE
85 Water Street
South Norwalk, CT 06854
203/852-7181
(Paints and finishes)

Decorative Painters

CHRISTIAN THEE &
ASSOCIATES
49 Old Stage Coach Road
Weston, CT 06883
203/454-0340
(Decorative artist)

DENNIS ROWAN
PAINTERS INC.
99 Franklin Street
Westport, CT 06880
203/227-6488
(Painters)

MIDDLESEX COUNTY
PAINTING CO.
4 Brainerd Avenue
Middletown, CT 06457
203/346-8848
*(Interior/exterior painting
contractors)*

THE POWER OF ONE
620 Washington Avenue
New Haven, CT 06457
203/772-9638
(General contractors/renovators)

ILLINOIS

ACCENT PRODUCTS
300 East Main Street
Lake Zurich, IL 60047
708/540-1604
*(Paints and graining and
combing tools)*

HIGHWOOD PAINT
AND HARDWARE
251 Waukegan Avenue
Highwood, IL 60040
708/432-1418
(Paint and decorating)

PRATHER PAINT &
WALLPAPER
101 Greenbay Road
Wilmette, IL 60091
708/251-6905
*(Paint, wallpaper, and
window treatments)*

MASSACHUSETTS

DIEMONT LEVY CO.
365 Albany Street
Boston, MA 02118
617/423-5580

EDGARTOWN PAINT
234 Upper Main Street
Edgartown, MA 02539
508/627-5112
(Paint)

HUBBARD PAINT
COMPANY
Dennisport Shopping Plaza
Dennisport, MA 02639
508/398-3600
(Paints and wallpaper)

NORMAN'S PAINT
505 Paradise Road
Swampscott, MA 01907
617/596-0345
(Paints and finishes)

THE OLD-FASHIONED
MILK PAINT CO.
436 Main Street
Groton, MA 01450
508/448-6336
(Milk-based paint)

NEW HAMPSHIRE

HAMILTON
DECORATING CENTER
18 Plaistow Road
Plaistow, NH 03865
603/382-9214
*(Paints, stencils, faux
finishes, brushes, and sponges)*

SAMRA'S PAINT
11 Lafayette Road
(Route 1)
North Hampton, NH 03862
603/964-6696
(Paints)

NEW JERSEY

BENJAMIN MOORE & CO.
51 Chestnut Ridge Road
Montvale, NJ 07645
201/573-9600
*(Interior/exterior paints and
supplies)*

COLOR FACTORY
The Donald Kaufman Color
Collection
114 West Palisade Avenue
Englewood, NJ 07631
201/568-2226
*(Interior paints, distributor of
designer paint lines, specially-
blended paints)*

EAGLE PAINT &
WALLPAPER
114 West Palisade Avenue
Englewood, NJ 07631
201/568-6051
(Paints and wallpaper)

GAIL GRISI
STENCILING, INC.
P.O. Box 1263
Haddonfield, NJ 08033
609/354-1757
(Stencils and supplies)

STENCILS ETC.
101 East Main Street
Moorestown, NJ 08057
609/866-2574
(Stencils, paints, and supplies)

Decorative Painter

DENIS CLEARY
270 Linden Avenue
Glen Ridge, NJ 07028
201/748-5976
(Painter)

NEW MEXICO

ECO DESIGN CO.
1365 Rufina Circle
Santa Fe, NM 87501
800/621-2591 or
505/438-3448
(Manufacturers and importers of natural/non-toxic paints and finishes)

LIVOS PLANT CHEMISTRY
1365 Rufina Circle
Santa Fe, NM 87501
800/621-2591 or
505/438-3448
(100% natural paints, finishes, and stains)

THE NATURAL CHOICE
1365 Rufina Circle
Santa Fe, NM 87501
800/621-2591 or
505/438-3448
(Low-toxic paints, stains, and waxes)

NEW YORK

C&W MERCANTILE
Main Street
Bridgehampton, NY 07631
516/537-7914
(Paints and wallpaper)

ELMONT PAINT & DECORATING
1604 Dutch Broadway
Elmont, NY 11003
516/825-2604
(Paints and decorating)

FIALA'S PAINT STORE
22-24 Railroad Avenue
Sayville, NY 11782
516/589-0949
(Paint)

GREAT NECK PAINT
29 Middle Neck Road
Great Neck, NY 11021
516/487-7380
(Paint)

LE ROY HOME DECORATING CENTER
66 Main Street
LeRoy, NY 14482
716/768-6455
(Paints and faux finishing)

SUN WALLPAPER & PAINT, INC.
47 Overocker Road
Poughkeepsie, NY 12603
914/471-2880
(Imported and domestic paints and finishes; lead abatement; spectrophotometer on premises)

New York City

GRACIOUS HOMES
1220 Third Avenue
New York, NY 10021
212/517-6300
(Paint and hardware supplies)

JANOVIC/PLAZA
30-35 Thomson Avenue
Long Island City, NY 11101
800/772-4381 or
718/392-3999
(Imported and domestic paints and brushes)

KREMER PIGMENTS, INC.
61 East 3rd Street
New York, NY 10003
212/995-5556
(Carries 500 pigments of historical and modern origins; full line of European brushes, lacquers and glues; 24-hr. turn-around time for mail order items)
Catalogue / Mail Order

MERIT-KAPLAN PAINT
237 East 44th Street
New York, NY 10017
212/682-3585
(Paint)

PEARL PAINT CO.
308 Canal Street
New York, NY 10013
212/431-7932
(Interior paints and artists'
supplies)

TERRA VERDE
120 Wooster Street
New York, NY 10012
212/925-4533
(Natural plant and mineral-
based paints from Germany,
domestic paints for chemically-
sensitive people)

Decorative Painters

AERO LIMITED
132 Spring Street
New York, NY 10012
212/966-1500
(Custom interiors)

ALEXANDER JULIAN
COLOURS
485 Fifth Avenue
New York, NY 10017
212/450-9213
(Color consultants)

CARLETON VARNEY
DESIGN GROUP
60 East 56th Street
New York, NY 10022
212/758-2810
(Custom interiors)

DONALD KAUFMAN
COLOR
410 West 13th Street
New York, NY 10014
212/243-2766
(Architectural color
consultants/custom color)

EVE ASHCRAFT
STUDIO
247 Centre Street
New York, NY 10013
212/966-1506
(Paint specialist, color
consultant)

GWATHMEY SIEGEL &
ASSOCIATES
ARCHITECTS
475 Tenth Avenue
New York, NY 10018
212/947-1240
(Architecture/interiors)

MARK HAMPTON, INC.
654 Madison Avenue
New York, NY 10021
212/753-4110
(Architecture/interiors)

PAXWELL PAINTING
STUDIOS
223 East 32nd Street
New York, NY 10016
212/725-1737
(Decorative painting and
murals)

OHIO

THE GLIDDEN CO.
925 Euclid Avenue
Cleveland, OH 44115
216/344-8000 or
800/221-4100
(Interior and exterior paints)

THE MARTIN
SENOUR CO.
101 Prospect Avenue
Cleveland, OH 44115
800/542-8468
(Antique color paints)

OREGON

PORTLAND PAINT &
SUPPLY
11025 N.E. Halsey Street
Portland, OR 97220
503/252-2440
(Paint and supplies)

PENNSYLVANIA

CHROMA ACRYLICS
205 Bucky Drive
Lititz, PA 17543
717/626-8866
(Artists' paints and mediums)

FINNAREN & HALEY
901 Washington Street
Conshohocken, PA 19428
215/825-1900 or
800/843-9800
*(Interior and exterior paints,
Victorian and historic colors,
and shades of '76)*

HENTOWN COUNTRY
STORE
Box 335, Peddler's Village
Lahaska, PA 18931
215/794-7096
*(Complete line of historic
colors and simulated whitewash)*

MARTIN/F. WEVER CO.
2727 Southampton Road
Philadelphia, PA 19154
215/677-5600
(Artists' paints)

OLD VILLAGE PAINT
P.O. Box 1030
Fort Washington, PA 19034
215/283-0200
*(Historic restoration house
and decorative paints)*

WASHINGTON

DALY'S
3525 Stone Way North
Seattle, WA 98103
206/633-4276
(Exterior and interior paints)

VERMONT

FINE PAINTS OF
EUROPE
P.O. Box 419
Route 4 West
Woodstock, VT 05091
802/457-2468 or
800/332-1556
*(High quality oil-based
interior and exterior house
paints from Holland, high-end
decorating and paint books)*
Catalogue / Mail Order

WISCONSIN

ROWE POTTERY
RETAIL STORE
217 West Main Street
Cambridge, WI 53523
608/423-3935
(Historic paints)

NATIONAL AND
INTERNATIONAL
LISTINGS

A.I. FRIEDMAN
44 West 18th Street
New York, NY 10011
800/736-5676 or
212/243-9000
(Art supplies)

BENJAMIN MOORE & CO.
51 Chestnut Ridge Road
Montvale, NJ 07645
201/573-9600 or
800/826-2623 for store
nearest you
(Paints)

HOME DEPOT
2727 Paces Serry Road
Northwest
Atlanta, GA 30339
404/433-8211 or
800/553-3199 for U.S.
listings
*(Interior and exterior paints
and supplies)*

JANOVIC/PLAZA, INC.
771 Ninth Avenue
New York, NY 10019
212/245-3241 for store
nearest you
*(Paints, windows, linens,
hardware, and general home
supplies)*

M. GRUMBACHER, INC.
30 Engelhard Drive
Cranbury, NJ 08512
609/655-8282
(Artists' paints and brushes)

PINTCHIK
278 Third Avenue
New York, NY 10010
212/777-3030 or
212/982-6600 for store
nearest you
(Discount home products and
paint)

POTTERY BARN
100 North Point
San Francisco, CA 94133
415/421-7900 or
800/922-9934 for
catalogue orders
(Decorative paints and
supplies)

SAM FLAX
12 West 20th Street
New York, NY 10011
212/620-3038 or
800/726-3529
(Paints)

THE SHERWIN
WILLIAMS CO.
101 Prospect Avenue
Cleveland, OH 44115
216/566-2000
(Paints and stains in colonial
colors)

TRU-TEST
MANUFACTURING CO.
201 Jandus Road
Cary, IL 60013
800/922-0061

CATALOGUE AND MAIL ORDER

DONALD KAUFMAN
COLOR COLLECTION
114 West Palisade Avenue
Englewood, NJ 07631
201/568-2226
(Top-of-the-line designer
colors)

LIBERTY PAINT
CATALOGUE, INC.
969 Columbia Street
Hudson, NY 12534
518/828-4060
(Faux finish brushes, tools,
sponges, and paints)

INTERNATIONAL LISTINGS

Canada

MONTREAL

PLACE BONAVENTURE
900 rue de la Gauchetière
Ouest
514/397-2355
(Design center)

ONTARIO

BENJAMIN MOORE & CO.
139 Mulock Avenue
Toronto M6N 1G9
416/766-1173
(Paints)

GRANNY TAUGHT US
HOW
RR4
Shelburne L09 1SO
519/925-2748
(Historic colors for country
decorating)

OLD PORT MARKETING
16050 Old Simcoe Road
Port Perry L9L 1P3
416/985-9744
(Distributor to retailers,
historic paints)

France

PARIS

BHV
52, rue de Rivoli
75004
42/74-90-00
(Household paint, brushes,
and wallpaper products)

BRICORAMA
8, avenue Porte d'Italie
75013
45/89-97-47
(Paint)

BRICOMIG–CATENA
94, avenue Denfert-
Rochereau
75014
43/35-11-99
(Paint)

Germany

AICHSTETTEN

DR. GEORG F. KREMER
Farbmühle
D-W-7974
7565/1011
(Carries 500 pigments of
historical and modern origins;
brushes, lacquers, and glues)
Catalogue / Mail Order

BODENTEICH

LIVOS
PLANTCHEMISTRY
D-3123
5825/8880
(Natural paints and finishes)

Great Britain

COLOURMAN PAINTS
Stockingate, Cotton
Clanford, Staffs
785/282799
(Own range of 24 matte, chalky
emulsion paints, colors matched
with 18th- and 19th-century
painted furniture; stock obscure
gums and pigments)

DEVON

NUTSHELL NATURAL
PAINTS
10 High Street, Totes
803/762-329 or 876-770
(Specialize in 20 natural
earth and mineral pigments
that can be used in any of
their paints)

LONDON

COLE & SON
18 Mortimer Street
WI
71/580-5369
(Wide range of paints,
emphasis in historic colors, and
hand block–print wallpapers)

CORNELLISEN & SON
105 Great Russell Street
WC1
71/636-1045
(Array of artist pigments and
materials)

E. PLOTON LTD.
273 Archway Road
N6
81/348-0315
(Specialists in paints, glazes,
and brushes)

GREEN & STONE LTD.
259 Kings Road
SW3
71/352-0837
(Fine art supplier: brushes,
paints, and stencils)

JOHN OLIVER PAINT
33 Pembridge Road
W11
71/221-6466
(Paints and wallpapers)

THE PAINT SERVICE
COMPANY LTD.
19 Eccleston Street
SW1
71/730-6408
(Specialists in paints, glazes,
and brushes)

PAPERS AND PAINTS
4 Park Walk
SW10
71/352-8626
(Specialists in historic paints
and colors)

THE STENCIL STORE
91 Lower Sloane Street
SW1
71/730-0728
(Wide range of stencils and
stencil paint supplies)

WARMINSTER

POTMOLEN PAINTS
27 Woodcock
Industrial Estate
985/213-960
(Traditional linseed oil paints, distempers, and limewashes)
Catalogue / Mail Order

Italy

MILAN

ADICOLOR SRL
Strada Provinciale 159
20060 Triginto di Mediglia
2/906-60740

AKZO COATINGS SPA
Via B. Croce 9
20090 Cesano Boscone
2/440-4241

COLORIFICIO CORTI
SPA
Via B. Luini 1
20035 Lissone
2/662-04860

ROME

CENTRO VERNICI
Via Visconte Maggiolo 14-18
00176
6/298-790

SIKKENS LINVEA SPA
Via Carciano 47
00131
6/419-1134

Japan

TOKYO

LOFT
21-1 Udagawa
Shibuya-ku
3/3462-0111
(Department store with paint and home supplies)

TOKYU HANDS
12-18 Udagawa
Shibuya-ku
3/5489-5111
(Department store with wide selection of do-it-yourself products)

ROOM SCHEMATICS

34 Warm off-white ceiling and trim, pale blue and medium blue walls
35 Warm off-white ceiling, pale golden yellow wall, medium golden yellow wall
38 Robin's-egg blue ceiling, warm pale gray walls, medium gray-green trim
39 Two shades of golden cream walls, white ceiling
42 Pale warm green wall, white with green tint ceiling and trim, warm pale gray floor
43 Pale and medium sage green in hall, deep rich brown floors, deep gray baseboards, golden ochre and venetian red walls, gray cream trim
46 Yellowed grays, pale and medium putty, warm cream walls, white trim
47 On farthest wall: pale ochre; side walls: venetian red and marble pink; trim: white

RESOURCES

Special thanks to Kremer Pigments Inc., NYC, for all paints, colors, and pigments pictured in this book.

QUOTES

ACKNOWLEDGMENTS

MANUFACTURER & RETAIL RESEARCH
Jeannette Durkan

QUOTE RESEARCH
Lige Rushing & Kate Doyle Hooper

ORIGINAL INTERVIEWS
Cynthia Stuart

AND SPECIAL THANKS TO: Connie Bang, Richard Bruce of the Middlesex County Painting Company, Lauren Clarke Caldwell, Amy Capen, Jin Chung, Ken Charbonneau of Benjamin Moore, Tony Chirico, Frank Cohen of Sun Wallpaper and Paint, Peter Colburn of Eco Design, M. Scott Cookson, Lauri Del Commune, Michael Drazen, Miki Duifterhof, Borden Elniff, Jane Friedman, Hayward Hill Gatling, Janice Goldklang, Charles Gwathmey, Mark Hampton, Meredith Harrington, Joanne Harrison, Patrick Higgins, Katherine Hourigan, Dina Dell'Arciprete-Houser, Andy Hughes, Pamela Hunt, Carol Janeway, Evan Janovic, Barbara Jones-Diggs, Alexander Julian, Donald Kaufman, Kremer Pigments, Nicholas Latimer, William Loverd, Barbara Lyon, Anne McCormick, Dwyer McIntosh, Sonny Mehta, Lan Nguyen, Ingrid Nystrom, Kumiko Ohta, Simon Rosenblum of Janovic/Plaza, Janet Rouber, Sandra Shea, Valerie Ebert Shiekman, Anne-Lise Spitzer, Meg Stebbins, Robin Swados, Aileen Tse, Rosa Villa, Shelley Wanger, Wayne Wolf.

COMMUNICATIONS

The world has gotten smaller and faster but we still can only be in one place at a time, which is why we are anxious to hear from you. We would like your input on stores and products that have impressed you. We are always happy to answer any questions you have about items in the book, and of course we are interested in feedback about Chic Simple.

Our address is:
**84 WOOSTER STREET
NEW YORK, NY 10012
FAX (212) 343-9678**
email address **info@chicsimple.com**
Compuserve number **72704,2346**

Stay in touch because "The more you know, the less you need."

KIM JOHNSON GROSS & JEFF STONE

COLOPHON

TYPE

The text of this book was set in two typefaces: New Baskerville and Futura.

The ITC version of **NEW BASKERVILLE** is called Baskerville, which itself is a facsimile reproduction of types cast from molds made by John Baskerville (1706–1775) from his designs. Baskerville's original face was one of the forerunners of the typestyle known to printers as the "modern face"—a "modern" of the period A.D. 1800. **FUTURA** was produced in 1928 by Paul Renner (1878–1956), former director of the Munich School of Design, for the Bauer Type Foundry. Futura is simple in design and wonderfully restful in reading. It has been widely used in advertising because of its even, modern appearance in mass and its harmony with a great variety of other modern types.

SEPARATION AND FILM PREPARATION BY

COLORSYSTEMS, INC.
New Britain, CT

PRINTED AND BOUND BY

BERTELSMANN PRINTING & MANUFACTURING CORP.
Berryville, Virginia

HARDWARE

Apple Macintosh Quadra 700 personal computers; APS Technologies Syquest Drives; Radius Precision Color Display/20; Radius 24X series Video Board; Hewlett Packard LaserJet 4, Supra Fax Modem

SOFTWARE

QuarkXPress 3.11, Adobe Photoshop 2.5.1, Microsoft Word 5.1, FileMaker Pro 2.0

MUSICWARE

(Love Gets Strange—The Songs of John Hiatt), Julee Cruise *(The Voice of Love)*, Smashing Pumpkins *(Siamese Twins)*, 10,000 Maniacs *(MTV Unplugged)*, The Sundays *(Blind)*, Jamiroquai *(Emergency on Planet Earth)*, Deep Forest *(Deep Forest)*, Rickie Lee Jones *(Traffic from Paradise)*, Mitchell Reid *(Save Me Sunday Morning)*, Bonnie Raitt *(Nick of Time)*, Lenny Kravitz *(Mama Said)*, Duke Ellington *(Solos, Duets, and Trios)*, The Chet Baker Quartet *(Cool Way to Heaven)*, Tori Amos *(Under the Pink)*, Real World *(Lament)*, DOS Records and 1993's Antone's *(Austin, Texas Rocking the Crossroads)*, Genes *(The Best of Reggae Sunsplash)*, Seal *(Seal)*

Special thanks to Cathy O'Brien of Capitol Records, Inc.

"Beauty of style and harmony and grace and good rhythm depend on simplicity."

PLATO